CAPE BUFFALO

BY LISA OWINGS

BELLWETHER MEDIA · MINNEAPOLIS, MN

This edition first published in 2012 by Bellwether Media, Inc.

No part of this publication may be reproduced in whole or in part without written permission of the publisher.
For information regarding permission, write to Bellwether Media, Inc., Attention: Permissions Department,
5357 Penn Avenue South, Minneapolis, MN 55419.

Library of Congress Cataloging-in-Publication Data

Owings, Lisa.
  The Cape buffalo / by Lisa Owings.
     p. cm. – (Pilot books. Nature's deadliest)
  Includes bibliographical references and index.
  Summary: "Fascinating images accompany information about the Cape buffalo. The combination of high-interest
subject matter and narrative text is intended for students in grades 3 through 7"–Provided by publisher.
  ISBN 978-1-60014-741-8 (hardcover : alk. paper)
  1. African buffalo–Juvenile literature. I. Title.
  QL737.U53O95 2012
  599.64'2–dc23
                                    2011033777

Printed in the United States of America, North Mankato, MN.

010112   1204

CONTENTS

Dangerous Crossing

The sun was about to set over Sabi Sand Game Reserve in South Africa. A group of seven men had just finished cutting down **acacia trees**. They were tired and ready to ride their tractor back to their lodge. But the tractor had broken down. They had no way of calling for help, so they decided to walk. They knew it would be dark soon.

On their way back to the lodge, they saw a herd of Cape buffalo crossing the road far ahead of them. They stopped and waited until the herd was out of sight. When they thought it was safe, they started walking again. None of the workers knew what awaited them on that dark road.

When the group came to the place where the buffalo had crossed, they were confronted by a deadly surprise. A huge **bull** was standing just a few feet away. And it was furious. The men scattered as the buffalo hurled itself toward them at full speed. Each climbed the nearest tree as fast as he could. Each hoped to escape the raging bull's monstrous horns.

But one of the men was too slow. The bull charged him. It pierced the man's stomach with its horns. Then the mighty beast tossed him over its back. The man landed hard behind the bull. To his horror, the bull turned around. It was ready to attack again.

Fortunately, the man landed in a hole. The bull shook its great horns. It tried again and again to **gore** the man. Finally, the bull gave up and walked away. The hole the man had landed in saved him from certain death. But his stomach was bleeding badly. Others in the group tied clothes around the wound. This helped to slow the bleeding and keep his intestines from falling out.

The group made it back to the lodge and flew the man to the nearest hospital. He survived the brutal attack. However, his troubles were not over. For months, the man suffered from infections caused by the bull's dirty horns.

Stronger than an Ox
A Cape buffalo is four times stronger than an ox. That is strong enough to tip a car!

Killer Cattle

Cape buffalo are among the largest and deadliest animals in Africa. They can weigh up to 2,000 pounds (900 kilograms) and reach speeds up to 35 miles (56 kilometers) per hour. Cape buffalo look calm while **grazing** on grasses. However, these animals charge the moment they feel threatened.

The Cape buffalo's most noticeable feature is its horns. Both males and females have hooked horns that can grow up to 4 feet (1.2 meters) long. They are deadly weapons against any predator. A bull's horns grow to cover his entire forehead in a protective shield. Even bullets often cannot get through this shield!

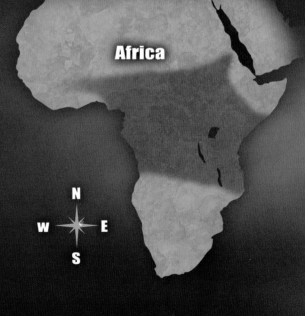

Africa

N
W E
S

Cape buffalo territory =

human Cape buffalo

Predator-Proof

Cape buffalo have few natural predators. Lions and crocodiles can sometimes catch calves or weak adults. However, a herd of angry Cape buffalo will attack these predators to defend their own kind.

11

A single Cape buffalo may be deadly. However, a herd of Cape buffalo is even more dangerous. A buffalo herd usually has between 50 and 500 animals. Herds of more than 2,000 buffalo are sometimes found. If one member of the herd is in trouble, the entire herd fights to protect it.

Cape buffalo are fierce fighters. They **trample** predators under their hooves. They gore them and toss them into the air with their hooked horns. They also ram into them with the full force of their weight. If a lion climbs a tree to escape, the buffalo will often stay beneath the tree for hours. They are ready to attack when the lion comes down!

Majority Rules

Some researchers believe female Cape buffalo vote to decide which direction the herd should move. As the herd rests, the females turn to face the direction they would like to travel. When it is time for the herd to get moving, the leader starts off in the direction most of the buffalo have "voted" for.

Bulls don't just fight to protect the herd. They also fight one another for **dominance**. A bull challenges another bull by tossing his head and showing off his horns. If the other bull accepts the challenge, the two begin to circle each other. Then they ram each other with their horns. The fight is usually over before either bull is killed.

The most dangerous bulls are **rogue** bulls. These are bulls that live on their own and do not have a herd to protect them. This means they are more likely to attack when they feel threatened. Many consider these unpredictable bulls to be the most dangerous animals in the world.

Born to Be Wild

The Cape buffalo is related to the water buffalo. People have tamed water buffalo and trained them to help with farm work. People have tried to tame Cape buffalo, but they are too dangerous. They will not cooperate with people.

Cape Buffalo Attacks

The Cape buffalo is one of the most popular animals for **big game hunting** in Africa. Its dangerous reputation, large size, and impressive horns attract hunters from all over the world. However, the Cape buffalo is very difficult and dangerous to kill. When it is hurt, its **adrenaline** begins to flow. Many people believe a wounded Cape buffalo is determined to kill.

The buffalo runs deep into the **brush**. It lies in wait for the hunter. When the hunter comes close, the buffalo attacks. It tramples the hunter into the ground with its sharp hooves. Many hunters call the Cape buffalo "Black Death."

People on a **safari** to see or hunt Cape buffalo can prevent an attack by taking a few simple precautions. The most important thing tourists can do when heading into Cape buffalo territory is listen to and follow the advice of their guide. The guide understands Cape buffalo body language and is usually armed.

Tourists should be aware of their surroundings at all times. Those who are not hunting should remain inside their vehicle. They should not make any sudden movements that could startle a buffalo. Hunters who do not kill a Cape buffalo with their first shot should wait for the buffalo to weaken before following it.

Birds and Buffalo

Oxpeckers and cattle egrets are birds that follow Cape buffalo herds. Cattle egrets eat the insects the buffalo disturb as they move through the grass. Oxpeckers eat pesky insects from the hides.

Disease, **habitat** loss, and hunting threaten Cape buffalo. The buffalo often catch diseases from livestock. They must compete with the livestock for space and food. A **rinderpest** outbreak in the 1980s killed many buffalo in Ethiopia, Sudan, Nigeria, and fifteen other African countries. Many people also hunt Cape buffalo for meat or trophies. Despite these threats, most Cape buffalo thrive in the protected areas of Africa.

Cape buffalo are important because their trampling and grazing make room for new plants to grow. Their droppings help **fertilize** the soil. Cape buffalo are also admired for the way they help and defend other members of their herd. By gaining a better understanding of Cape buffalo, we can feel safer sharing the savannahs with these wild and unpredictable animals.

Attack Facts

- Cape buffalo kill around 200 people every year in Africa.

- Cape buffalo are said to have killed more big game hunters than any other animal.

Glossary

acacia trees—small trees with thorny leaves that grow in warm parts of the world

adrenaline—a chemical the body produces when it needs more energy or senses danger

big game hunting—a sport in which hunters try to kill large, dangerous animals

brush—small trees and shrubs

bull—a male Cape buffalo

dominance—power or control over someone or something

fertilize—to make capable of supporting plant growth

gore—to pierce

grazing—feeding on grasses and plants

habitat—the environment in which plants and animals usually live

rinderpest—a disease that kills cattle

rogue—a bull that has left the herd because he can no longer compete with the other buffalo in the herd

safari—a trip to see or hunt wildlife in their natural habitats

trample—to damage or crush something by walking over it

To Learn More

At the Library

Gibbs, Maddie. *African Buffalo*. New York, N.Y.: PowerKids Press, 2011.

Hadithi, Mwenye. *Bumping Buffalo*. London, U.K.: Hodder Children's Books, 2011.

Marsh, Carole. *The Rip-Roaring Mystery on the African Safari*. Peachtree City, Ga.: Carole Marsh/Gallopade International, 2011.

On the Web

Learning more about Cape buffalo is as easy as 1, 2, 3.

1. Go to www.factsurfer.com.

2. Enter "Cape buffalo" into the search box.

3. Click the "Surf" button and you will see a list of related Web sites.

With factsurfer.com, finding more information is just a click away.

Index

The images in this book are reproduced through the courtesy of: John Warburton-Lee Photography / Photolibrary, front cover; Nick Garbutt / Photolibrary, pp. 4-5; Ted Miller / Photolibrary, pp. 6-7; Anup Shah / naturepl.com, pp. 8-9; Dolder W / Photolibrary, p. 11; Pete Oxford / Getty Images, pp. 12-13; Anup Shah / Minden Pictures, pp. 14-15; Martin Applegate, pp. 16-17; Denny Allen / Getty Images, pp. 18-19; Ingo Arndt / Minden Pictures, p. 21.